EXPLODE
YOUR INCOME
WITH
BETTER
REAL ESTATE PHOTOS

HOW TO TAKE PHOTOS THAT WILL CONNECT WITH YOUR BUYER, MAKE YOUR SELLER THINK YOU'RE A ROCK STAR, AND MAKE YOU MORE MONEY NOW!

CONTENTS

INTRODUCTION

The world has changed. They way people shop for and buy property has changed. Once upon a time, buyers would lean heavily on the real estate agent to find a home that fits their needs, desires, budget, and so forth. A buyer might walk into a real estate agent's office and trust the agent to find what they are looking for and not do a whole lot of homework beyond some ads in the newspaper. Those days are long gone.

Today, buyers do their own research. They look up their own properties. They largely make their own choices on what properties to visit in person. Websites like Zillow and Realtor.com have made buyers much more active in the process and, as such, the need to market directly to the buyer on an emotional level is now more important that it ever has been. This marketing starts BEFORE the buyer ever makes contact with a real estate agent. The final sale (or at least the emotional attachment) is now often made in the buyers living room in the middle of the night instead of when walking through the property for the first time.

With these new realities, it is absolutely critical that the photography work on homes for sale be as amazing as possible. There is no doubt that a high quality, professional photo will get a buyer attached to a home in a way that a poor photo never could. This is the first impression and is more important than any other amount of data written in the listing. If the photos are terrible, you will have a very hard time getting them to care about any of the text or written data listed (but they might wonder if they can low ball you on the offer). On the other hand, if the photos are amazing and they start to fall in love, they'll look at all the rest of the information to find the facts they need to justify buying the home even if it is above their budget. People make buying decisions with emotions and justify them with facts. The photos can take advantage of this human trend on your behalf, or it can sabotage you.

If you apply the 21 principles written in this book, you WILL improve your real estate photos. In turn, you will make more money and have happier clients in the industry. This will be true both for the real estate agent and the real estate photographer.

This book is written both for the real estate agent who wants to take their own photos as well as the real estate photographer. In some of the chapters, I'll be speaking more toward the real estate agent and in others I'll be speaking more toward the real estate photographer. It should be fairly obvious at the time whom the primary target is. Regardless, the information is relevant to both.

Every real estate listing should have a professional real estate photo-shoot. Even if you as the real estate agent are going to be the one physically doing this, you should still be doing professional quality work. This book will guide you in this.

HIRE A PROFESSIONAL

Perhaps the most important way to improve your real estate photography, is to hire a professional photographer.

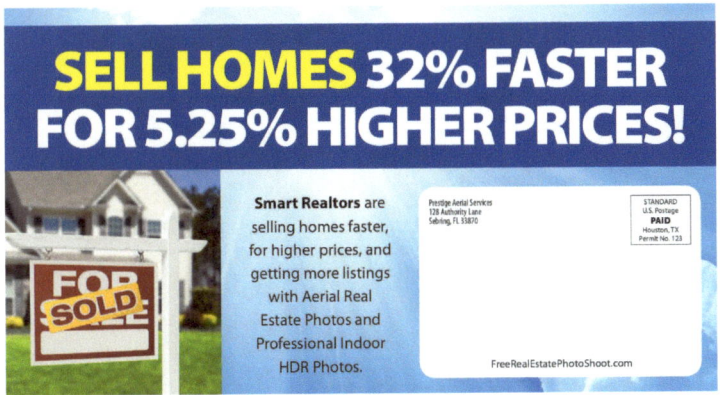

Why would I include this? After all, isn't the whole point of this book to give you tools and tricks so you can shoot your own listings?

Well, to a point, yes. However, all the reading in the world will not change the fact that to properly learn how to apply this knowledge will require practice . . . and a lot of it if you want to do it well. You then need to ask yourself, what's the best use of your time? What activities will make you the most money? If you answer that question honestly, I think you will have to admit that taking real estate photos is not on the list.

If you're a real estate agent, you make money by putting up new listings and finding buyers for those listings. There is no doubt that high quality, professional Interior HDR and Aerial Photos will greatly help. However, there is no need for you to personally spend your time photographing a home. Quite frankly, you'll make a lot more money by paying a professional Real Estate Photographer to perform the photo shoot than you would if you spend the many hours learning to master the skill yourself (not to mention the thousands of dollars you'll save on equipment).

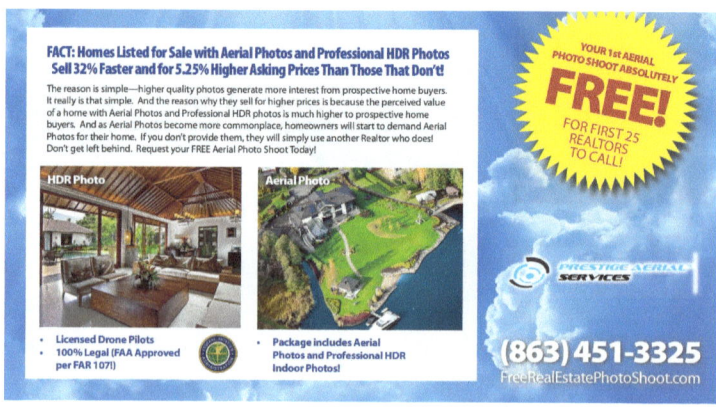

And don't forget, if you are going to incorporate aerial photography (and you're leaving money on the table of you do not), you're going to need to hire a licensed drone pilot/photographer anyway unless you intend to also spend the time and money to become an FAA certified drone pilot yourself.

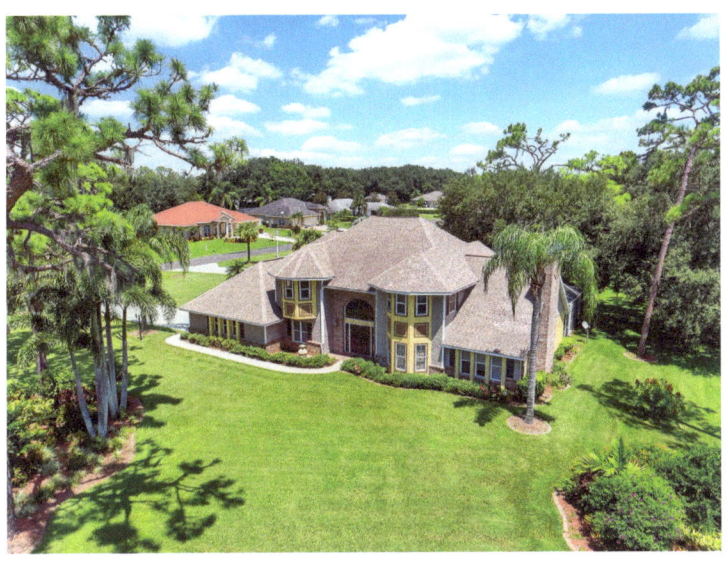

One of the greatest enhancements that you now have in regards to how you market your properties is the ability to add aerial photography to your real estate pictures. Just a few years ago, aerial photography was reserved for only the highest end listings due to the extreme cost of sending a photographer to the site in an airplane or helicopter. Now, with the recent advancements in drone technology, every listing on the market can enjoy the benefits of aerial photography. So, what are those benefits?

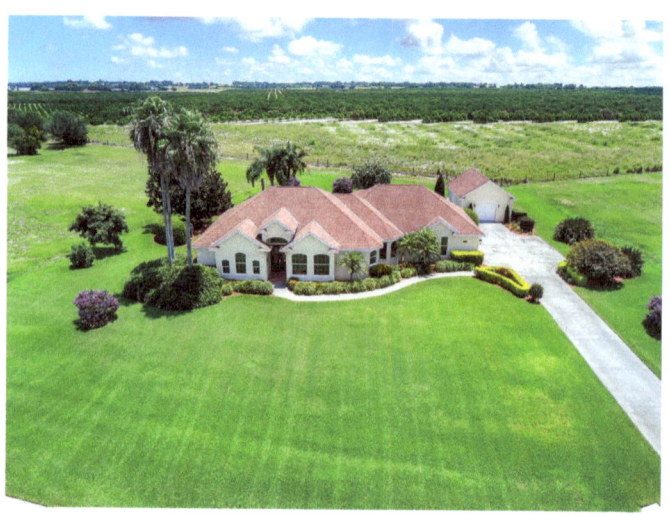

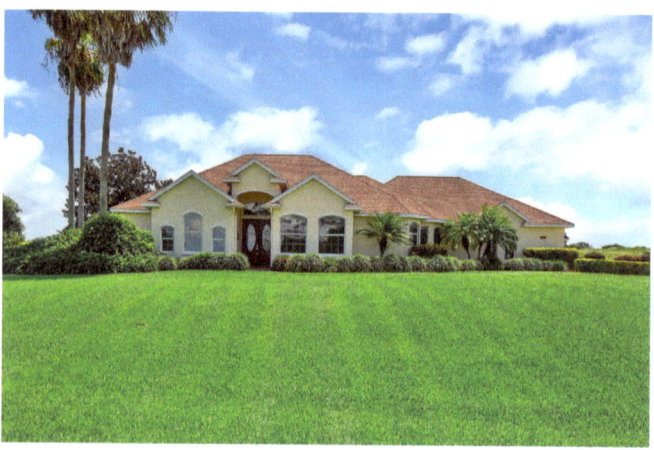

A study published a few years ago by the Sky Eye Network found that adding aerial photos to professional HDR photos will result in homes selling 32% FASTER and for 5.25% HIGHER selling prices. In addition, the real estate agent will normally get more listings when they tell sellers at a listing appointment that they will market their home with aerial photos.

Now, if you've got this idea that you can just go to the local Walmart and pick up a cheap drone with a camera, you've got another thing coming. There are some very important legal and practical things you need to know before you can do this.

DRONES ARE AIRCRAFT! As such, you have to have a specific pilot certification from the FAA to legally fly them for any reason other than pure hobby. So, if you are marketing a real estate listing, you are NOT flying for pure hobby and thus need the certification under Part 107 of the Federal Aviation Regulations. Failure to do so can result in fines that go into the 5 figures.

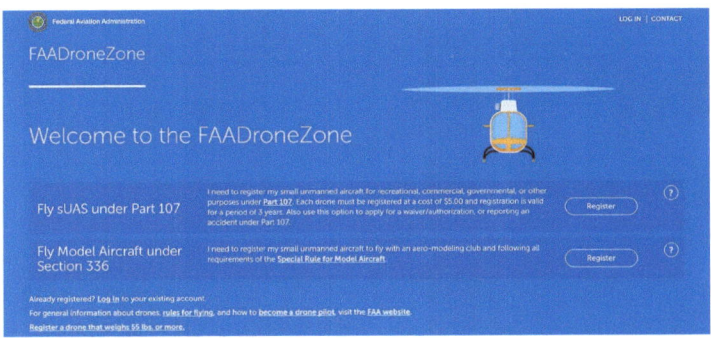

Once you obtain your FAA Part 107 drone pilot certificate, you will be able to legally take your own aerial photos. Be sure to get a good quality aircraft. At the time of this writing, DJI has, by far, the largest market share of drone aircraft. If you're not sure what to get, DJI is probably your best bet (again, as of 2019). For real estate photography, you don't need a $30,000 aircraft. Rather, spending about $1000 (plus or minus) on an aircraft in the Mavic or Phantom series will normally work just fine.

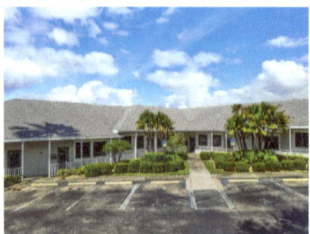
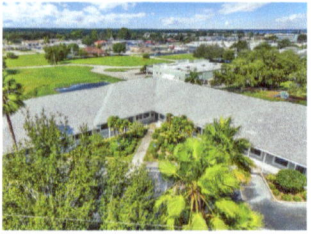
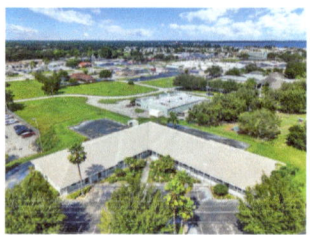

When you first start doing this, it would be in your interest to take a lot of aerial photos at the site. Start at the front at about roof level and take a picture, then fly back and climb to 40–50 feet or so and take another picture. Then fly back and climb to 200–300 and take another photo. Continue this process until you have at least 3 photos of each side and each corner from different altitudes (personally, I like my corner shots to be more like angled front and back shots in most cases). After you finish taking the side and corner photos, fly above the house and take a bird's eye view looking straight down.

The above instructions will yield a lot of photos. From these, you will be able to select 4 or 5 good ones to edit and develop for the listing. In time, you will learn which views you like best and be able to reduce the number of photos you take on site, but until you reach that point, following these instructions will help ensure an acceptable result.

One final tip for taking the aerial photos, it's not too uncommon to have a home that has trees right in the spot where your drone needs to be for an awesome aerial photo. So . . . what do you do when this happens?

What normally works well is to get under the trees. Climb (very carefully) as high as you can and take a photo. If there are a lot of trees, expect to take multiple photos to make sure you can find shots that will work. While you sometimes will not be able to get a true obvious aerial perspective, this is still highly effective because it changes the perspective of the view. Often times, the buyer may not be conscious of what is different, yet they will pick up on the difference even if just on a subconscious level. As a result, your listing will still stand out from your competitors and you will get better results than if you skipped the aerials.

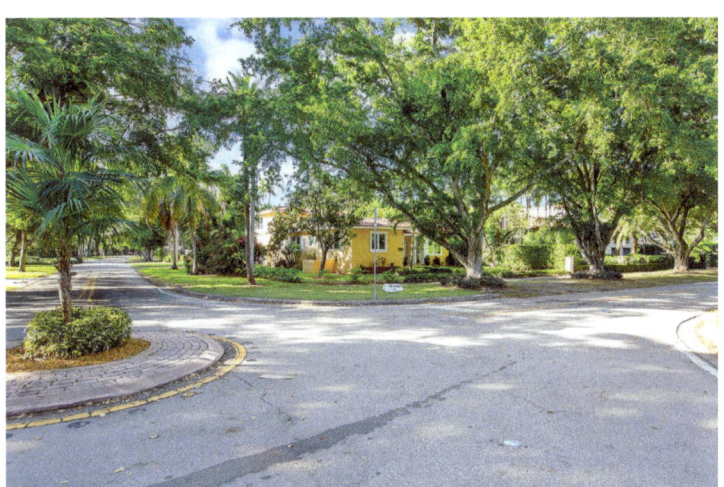

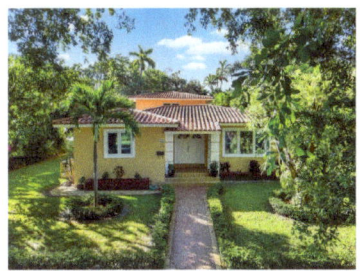
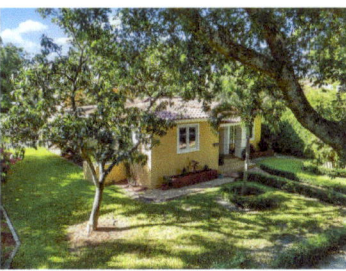

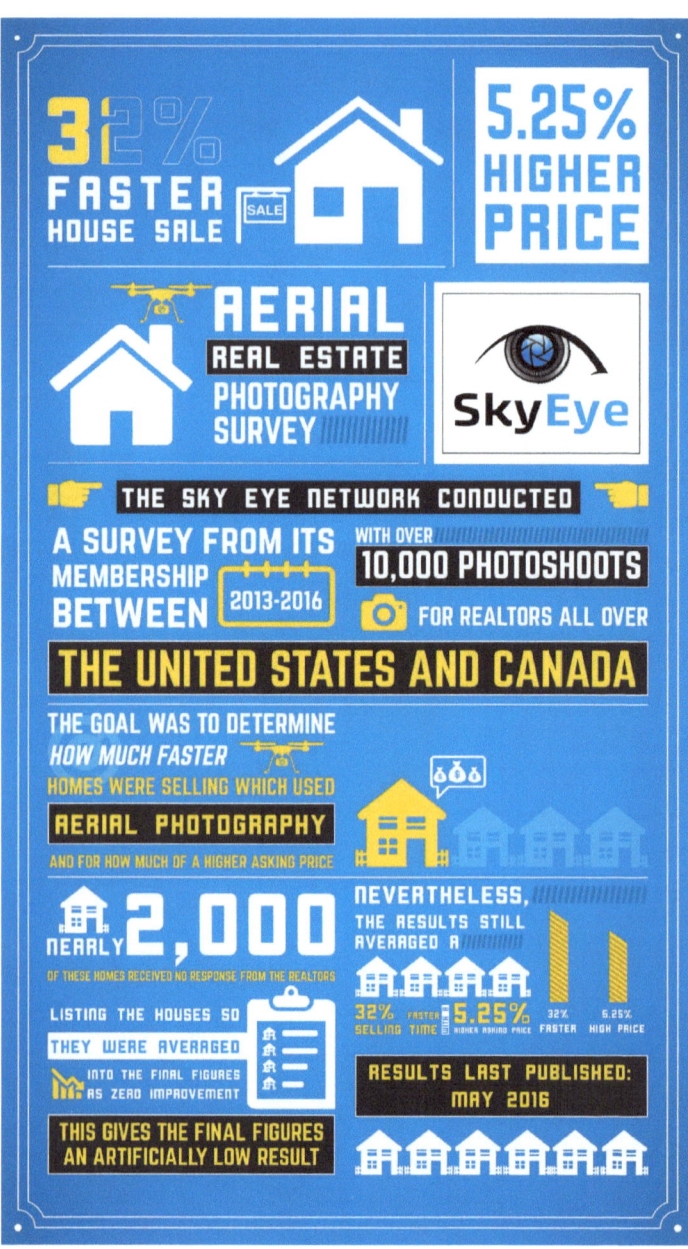

USE A FULL FRAME DSLR

I'm not going to lie to you, this one's expensive. But if you want to take your photography work to the next level, it's worth the investment. However, considering the price tag, it's yet another reason to consider hiring a professional to handle your real estate shoots.

I won't bore you with technical details, but a DSLR is a professional grade camera. Some of these can be obtained on a small budget, but a full frame DSLR (with a high-quality lens—also very important) is going to run thousands of dollars. Expensive? Yes! But remember, you get what you pay for. You're going to use this to take the most critical photos of the entire listing. After your aerial photos draw them in, these will be the ones that make them fall in love and want to buy the house before they even reach out to you to schedule a time to see the property.

This book is not intended to go into extreme technical detail between full frame and other types of DSLR's. However, just know that a full frame is going to yield better results, especially in low light environments.

While there are exceptions for everything, you normally do not want to use a flash or other professional lighting on a standard real estate shoot. One of the ideas is to replicate what the human eye will actually see and much of this is lost if you are using light other than what the house already has or sunlight that can come in through the windows. This means that some rooms WILL be darker than desired for photography purposes (not to mention that sometimes the power will be out at vacant properties). When this happens, the full frame DSLR will still yield amazing results. I've taken some photos in rooms so dark you could barely see your hand in front of your face. When it was all done, it looked like the lights were on.

TAKE BRACKETED (HDR) PHOTOS

This is absolutely key! You'll remember I previously said that homes listed with aerial photos AND professional HDR photos sell an average of 32% FASTER and for 5.25% HIGHER prices. What I didn't mention is, what is HDR photography?

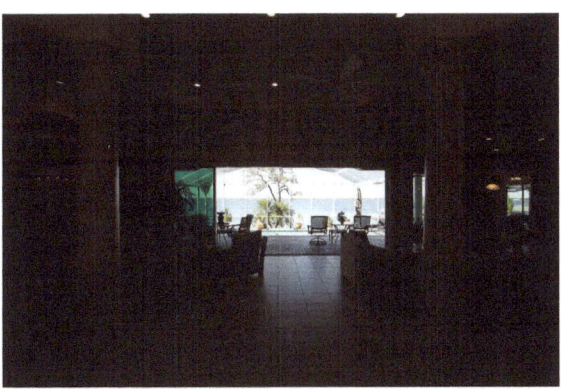

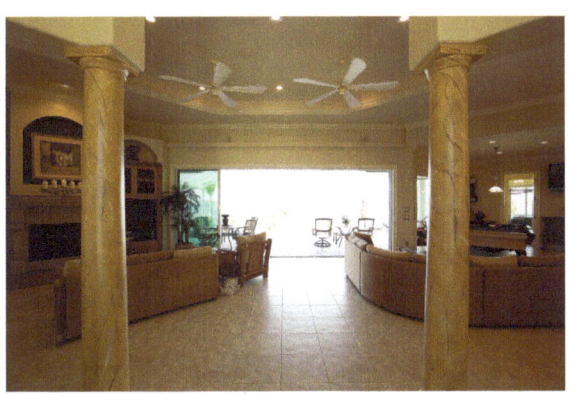

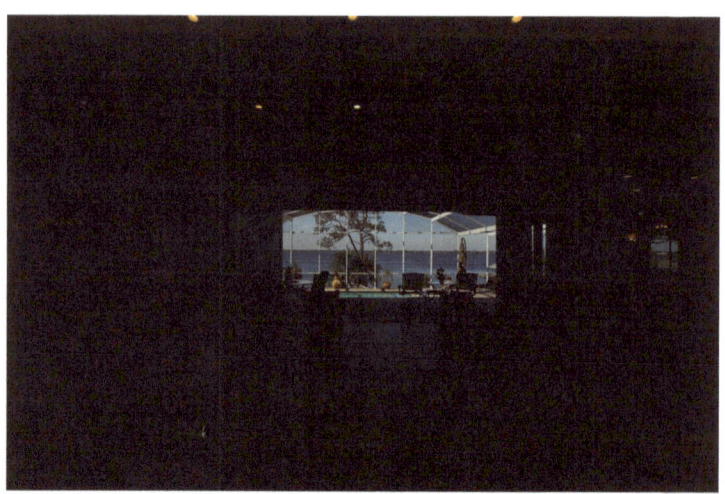

HDR photography is a technique of taking multiple photos at different exposures and combining them together in post-production for a stunning final result.

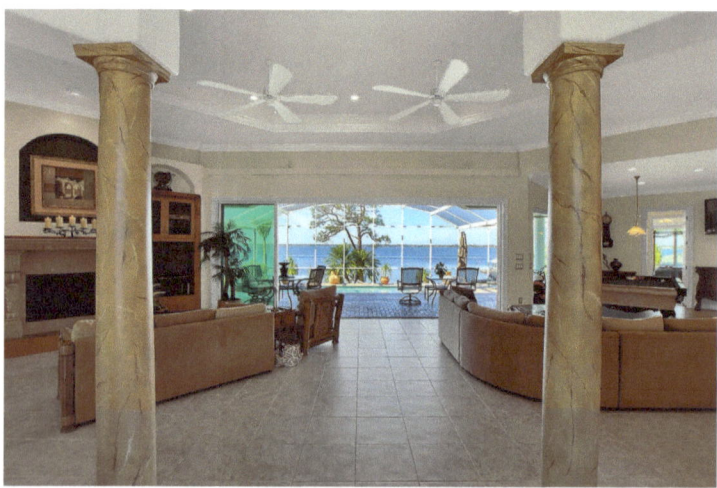

Here's the idea. With as much as camera technology has advanced today, its ability to image and compensate for light difference is still not as advanced as the human eye. This is why you can take a picture of a room and find the windows are totally blown out. Or, you can take a picture of the same window, properly exposed, and then find that the room is now totally dark. HDR (High Dynamic Range) photography is how we can get past this.

For an interior real estate shoot, you need to take 3 photos. One should be over exposed (very bright), one under exposed (very dark) and one exposed normally (I personally set my stops at −3, 0, and +3). In post-production, you will use the best parts of each photo to create your final result. For example, the under exposed photo is often way too dark for the room, but the view out the window often looks great.

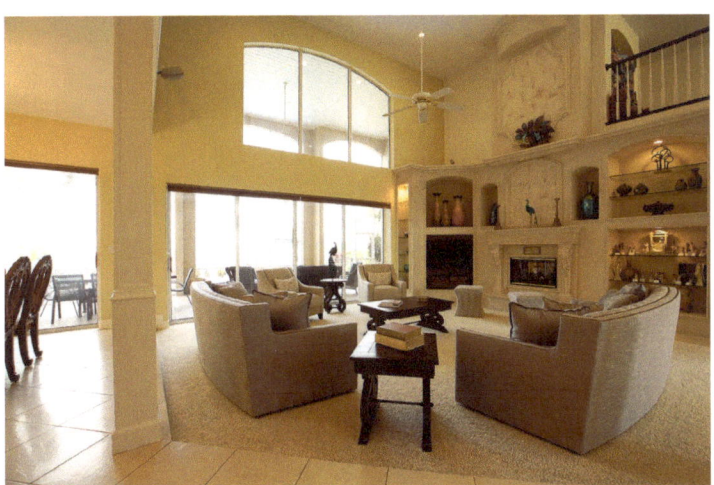

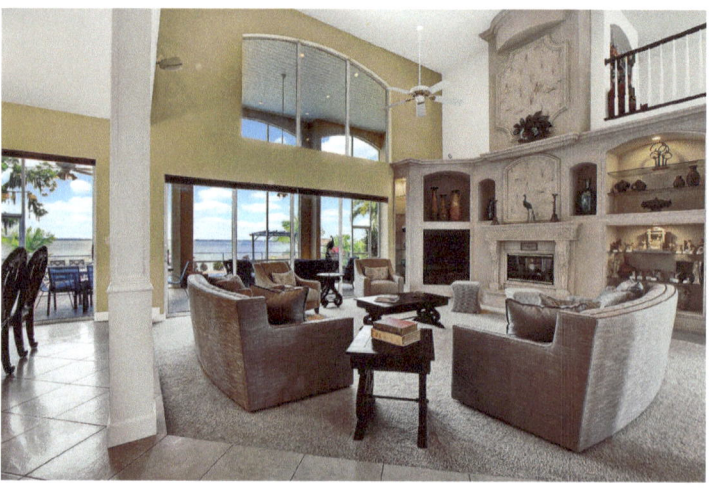

There are several ways to merge these photos, some manual and some automatic. For the software approach, Adobe products such as Lightroom and Photoshop can merge them together. In addition, programs like Photomatix will merge many photos together in a "batch" which will save some time. Ideally, you're going to want a combination of auto and manual techniques to get the best result.

Many cameras actually have an HDR option built in which is supposed to do much of this for you, but I do not suggest this on a professional shoot. You will get a much better result merging the photos in post-production.

LEARN BASIC PHOTO EDITING

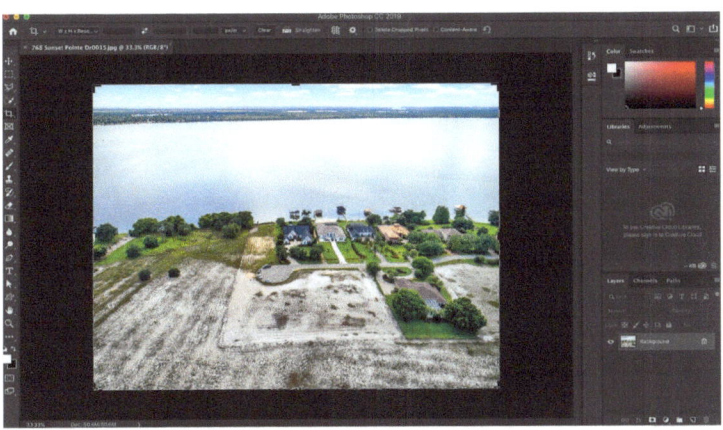

I'd like to stress that I am suggesting you learn BASIC photo editing. If you want to go deeper into that because you enjoy it, great! However, if for business purposes alone, your time will be more profitable focusing on revenue generating activities than it would learning the ins and outs of photo editing. You can hire a photo editor for that.

However, there are a few skills that are good to know primarily because it is often faster to make the quick edit than to explain to an editor what you want done in a single photo.

The primary editing skill I suggest you learn is how to remove simple objects. This can be done in Photoshop (and several other programs as well). Even using a good photo editor, you should expect that objects that should be removed will, from time to time, get overlooked and will thus remain in the photo. There are enormous amounts of things a good photo editor will be doing to each picture and it's not reasonable to expect everything to be perfect 100% of the time (a good editor will get close to that, but nobody's perfect).

Complicated object removals will still need to be sent back to the editor. However, simple objects (like part of the tripod leg that was caught in a reflection) can often be removed in less time that it would take to explain to the editor what needs to be done. The fact that it is sometimes faster to do something simple than to send it back out is the only reason I suggest you learn this basic skill.

HIRE A PHOTO EDITOR

If you're a real estate agent, the reasons for this are probably obvious based on the last chapter. However, if you're a photographer, you might be surprised to know I suggest this to you as well. Why???

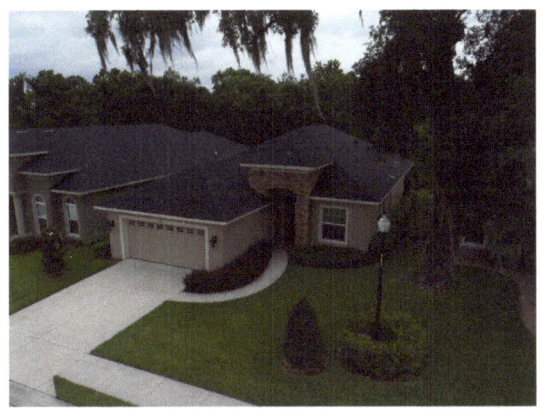

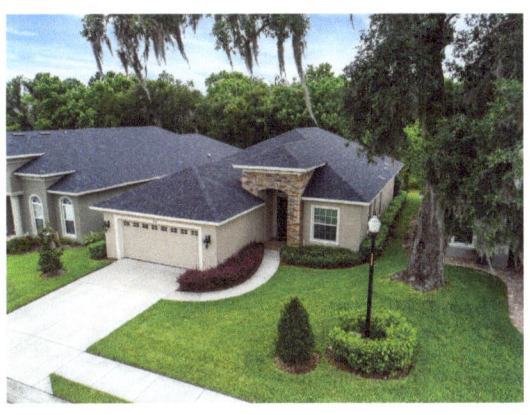

When I was getting started in the real estate photography business, I took a class from a photographer that did a lot of high-end work (his shoots run thousands of dollars per shoot—that high end). When he arrived at the part of the course that dealt with editing and retouching, he suggested that we not get involved with it personally and to hire an editor. The class then proceeded to have his photo editor explain the process and how they work together to create a stunning final result.

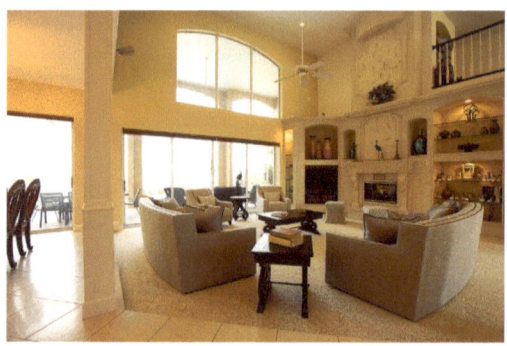

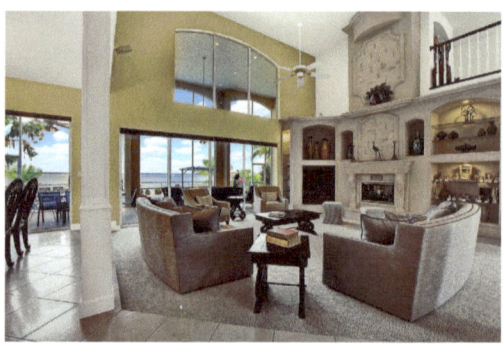

Taking awesome real estate photos is an art. In the same way, editing a real estate photo is also an art, but the skill set is different. No matter how hard you try, if you spend your days shooting and then try to edit those few shoots in the evening or the next day, you will not be as good as someone who does nothing but edit photos day in and day out. Plus, if you are shooting all day, when exactly are you going to have the time to edit the photos (and do it properly)?

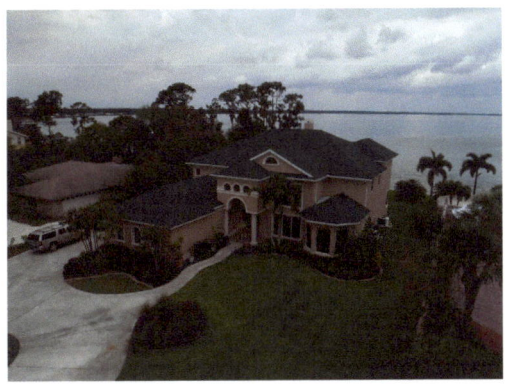

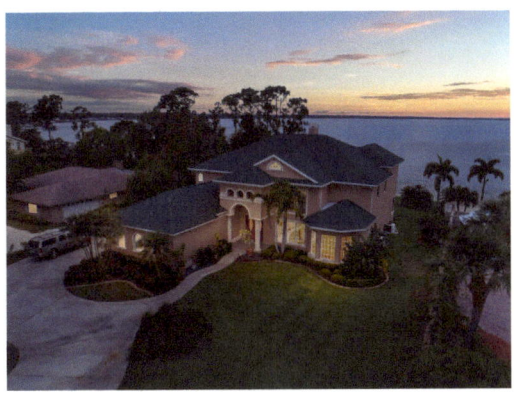

Teaming up with a talented photo editor will allow you to focus on taking pictures and developing that skill while you editor focus on doing the post production. Have both parties focusing on their specialties will yield a much better result than doing everything yourself.

LOWER YOUR TRIPOD

With this title, I guess it goes without saying that I would suggest you USE a tripod. This will be a requirement when you shoot bracketed (HDR) photos. These photos must all line up with each other in post-production for it to work, and the exposure times used for the interior photos will be too long to hold the camera steady by hand.

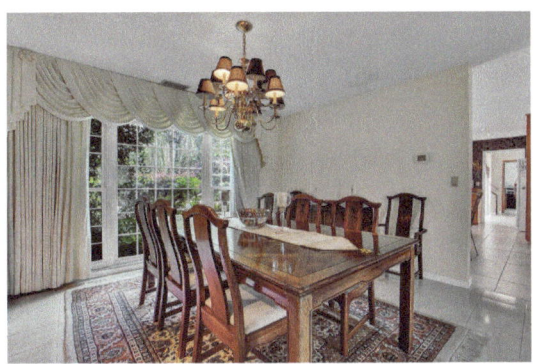

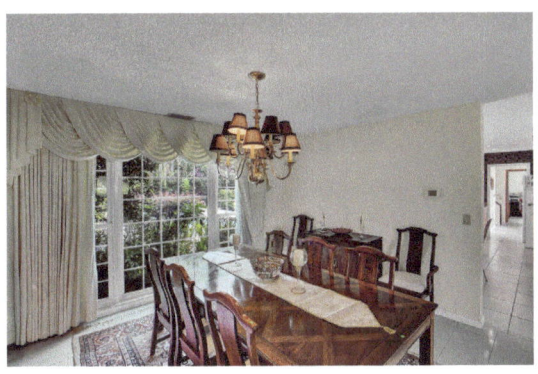

One of the telltale signs that tips me off to the fact that the realtor either took their own photos (not professionally done) or the photographer is a rookie is the height of the photos. Almost everyone starts taking pictures near eye level throughout the house (I'll admit . . . I did this too). This is a mistake. Correcting it is probably one of the best ways to quickly make your photos look like there were handled by a professional.

So, why does this even matter? Well, there's a couple reasons. The most logical is it allows more of the floor to be in the photo without taking away any practical "space" that's in the room. In other words, the buyer sees more of the room while making it look just as large and sometimes maybe even a bit larger. Second, it changes the perspective to a level that is more in line with how a space will be experienced. For example, someone relaxing in a living room is not going to see the room at eye level at that moment. They will be lower, sitting on the couch. These perspective changes help the buyer connect emotionally with the room in the photo and thus make the house more desirable.

While that's a practical reason why lowering the tripod is important, I think there's another reason. Now, I don't have any data or studies to back up this up, but I believe one of the reasons lowering the tripod makes a difference is because high-end real estate and architectural photography that people see in magazines is normally photographed from a lower perspective. As a result, when people see real estate photos framed the same way, their mind connects those photos with ones they've seen in the past that were clearly done by highly paid professionals.

So that covers a bit about why you should lower your tripod when taking the pictures. However, that still leaves the larger question, how low should you lower it?

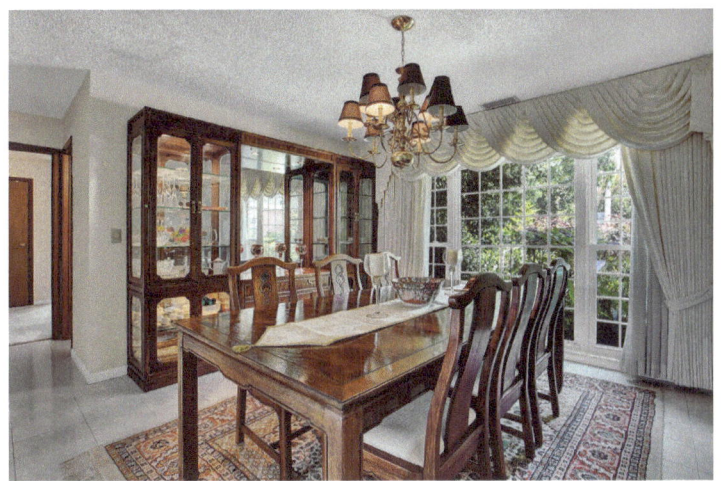

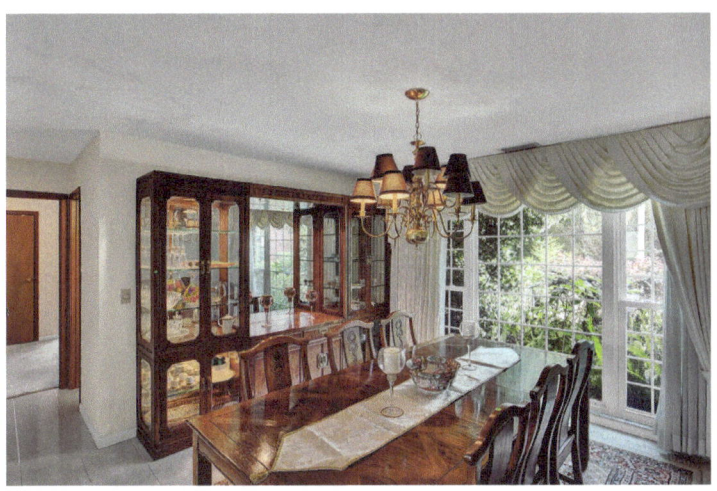

I'll start big picture and then try to narrow it down a bit. There's no doubt that there is a certain amount of art to this, but there are some general principles that can guide you as well. Remember, most nonprofessionals are taking their photos too high, so you don't need this to be perfect to give you a much more professional look.

A general rule of thumb (for interior photos) is if you are shooting a large room, put the tripod about chest level. In a smaller room, like a bedroom, lower it to just about the height of the door handle.

A principle that's a little more specific, look at the top of the primary flat surface. In a bedroom, this is normally the bed. In a kitchen or bathroom, normally the counter. Lower the tripod until the camera is just slightly above this surface. You should be able to see the entire top of the counter or bed, but about as low as possible and still be able to do this.

Finally, another principle that works just about everywhere else, lower the camera to the level that the room will be experienced. What does this mean? Well, if you're in a living room, for example, put the camera at what would be eye level for people sitting on the couch in the room.

Again, the exact height of the tripod is a bit of an art and personal preference and style does come into play. Work hard on always gauging this better on each shoot, but don't lose too much sleep over getting it perfect at the start. Remember, nonprofessionals will almost ALWAYS take the photo from eye level, so lowering it in any way will likely make your photos look more professional.

AVOID "DEAD SPACE"

Okay, this one will work to put you above many professionals. Even those taking real estate photos for a living include "dead space" in their photographs. The result is they needlessly make the room look smaller. I suppose what's desirable changes with the culture and with time, but today, people like to see open space and large rooms. So, if your photos don't maximize the room size, you are taking away from the perceived value of the home in the eyes of the buyer. Why would you ever do this?

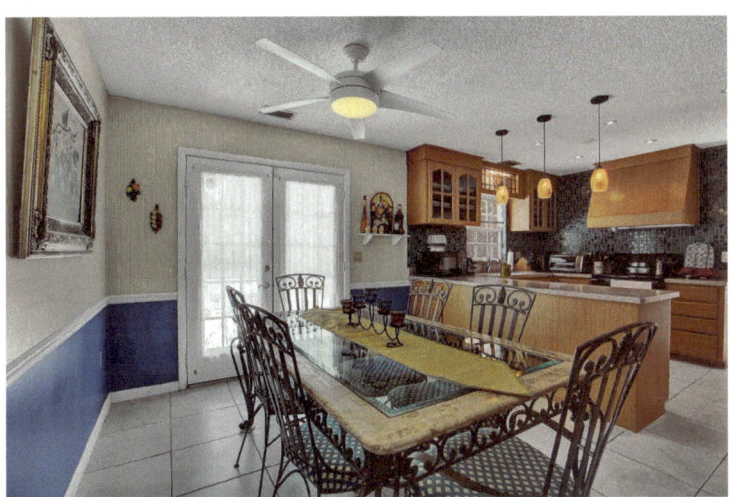

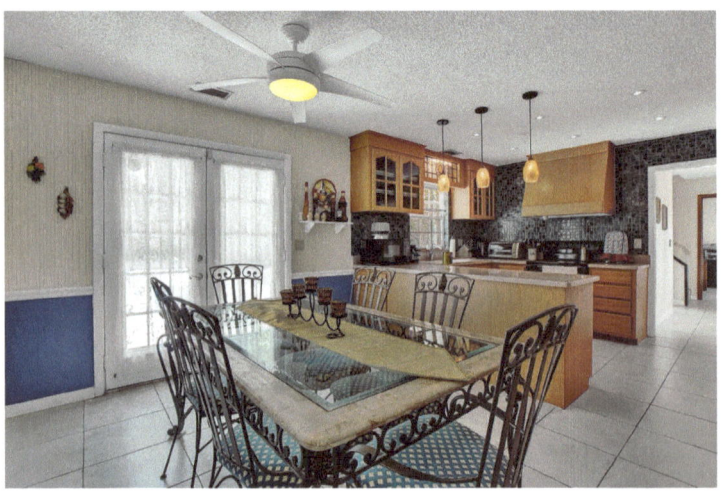

Okay, so before I explain how to avoid dead space, I should probably define it for you. Dead space is any part of a photo that is taken up by a wall or other obstruction that does not add any necessary detail or information to the image.

Taking pictures with dead space often happens when shooting from a corner. As will be discussed later in the book, taking pictures from corners is a good thing, BUT AVOID THE DEAD SPACE!

The way this normally happens is the photographer is shooting from the corner looking toward the opposite side of the room. While the 2 walls on the far end will be in view, the 2 walls that make up your corner, in most cases, should not. However, many photographers will include part of one of these walls in the photo and it will take up perhaps 10–20% of one side of the picture.

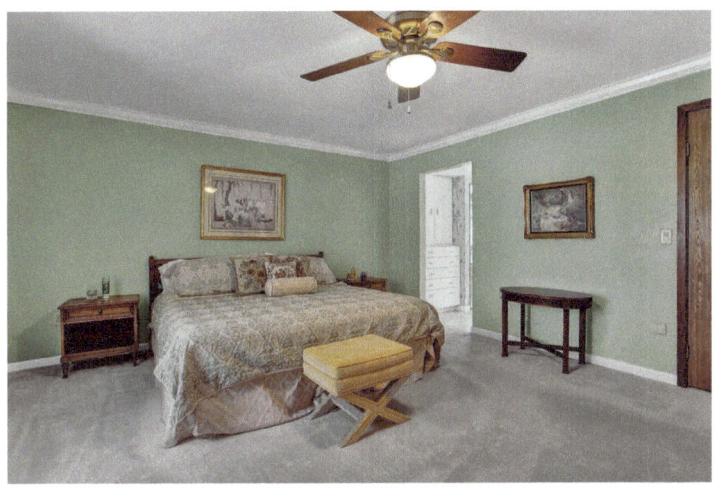

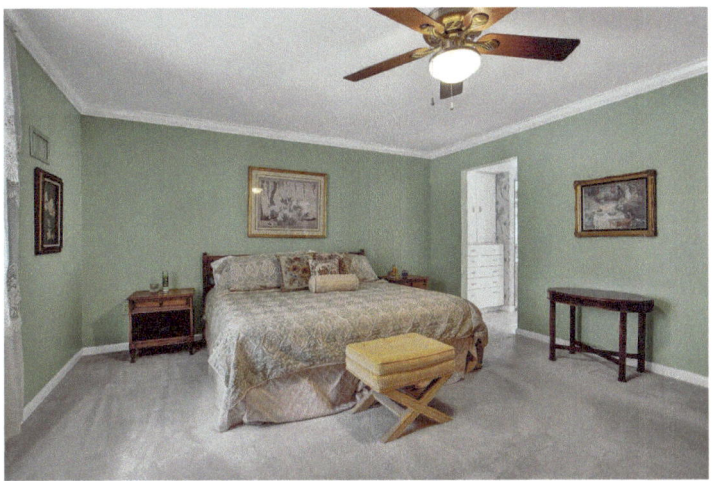

In the worse cases, there is nothing to be seen here but wall and you are losing as much as 20% of your open space with nothing gained. This is why I call it "dead space". It contributes nothing and it makes the room look smaller.

Now, it's true that there are some cases where letting in some of the wall adds to the photo. Perhaps it's needed to include a piece of furniture that you want in the photo. Perhaps the layout of the room prevents you from removing it totally. However, in the vast majority of cases, it hurts your photo more than it helps and should normally be avoided.

STAGE THE HOME

There are few things that puzzle me more than to arrive at the home of a seller to take their pictures and find the inside a complete train wreck. Personally, I lay this squarely on the feet of the sellers (not the agent). The agent is working for a commission on the sale which is not enough to be expected to include maid service. The seller, on the other hand, almost always has a 6-figure transaction they are working toward. Considering the dollar amount on even a small home, why would you not have the home 110% ready for shooting on the day of the photo shoot? With buyers starting their search on the internet, the photography is probably the most important event in regards to building the marketing package for the home!

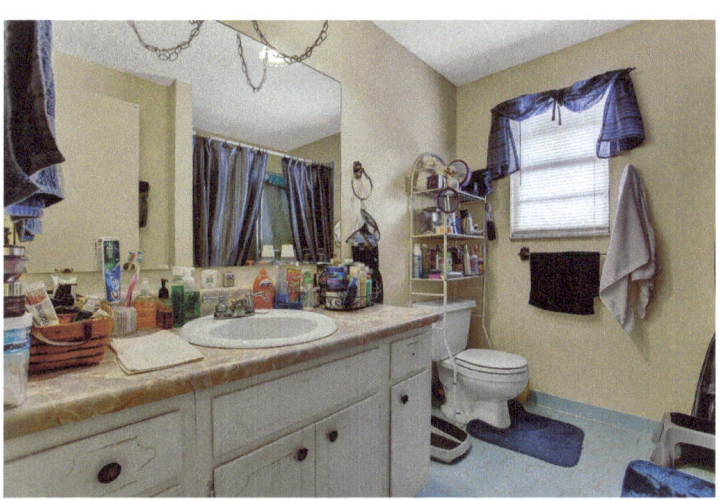

If you're reading this book, you're probably already in full agreement with the above paragraph. If you're an agent, you've probably shook your head and bit your tongue more than once at the condition a seller kept their house in (and then still wanted you to sell it 50% above market value, in 7 days or less, closing just a fast—a little sarcasm, but . . . you know). So, I think I can end that rant there. That said, there is still more to talk about staging.

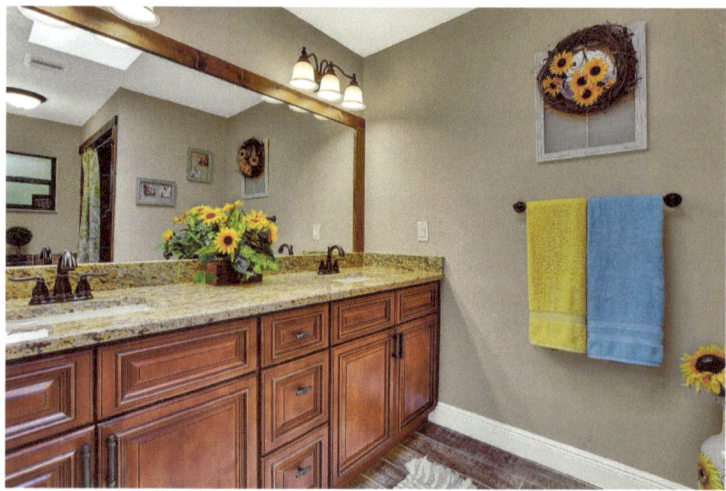

There is a difference between a clean house and one that is staged for selling. I remember years ago, when selling the first house I purchased, we hired a professional stager to coach us in preparing our home. She gave us a very detailed report of what exactly we needed to do, many things we would not have thought of (like take down family pictures), and we then followed her instructions before putting the house on the market. The result? We sold the house in 1 day above asking price!

Following the instructions in this book WILL improve your real estate photos. However, the condition and staging of the home at the time of shooting will play a large role as well. When I'm on a job site, I can take pretty pictures of a dump all day long . . . but it's still a dump.

Ultimately, I'm a big fan of hiring professionals. Along this line, I would encourage any seller to contact and hire a professional stager to prepare the home either by having the stager do all the work, or writing a detailed report which the seller can then carry out.

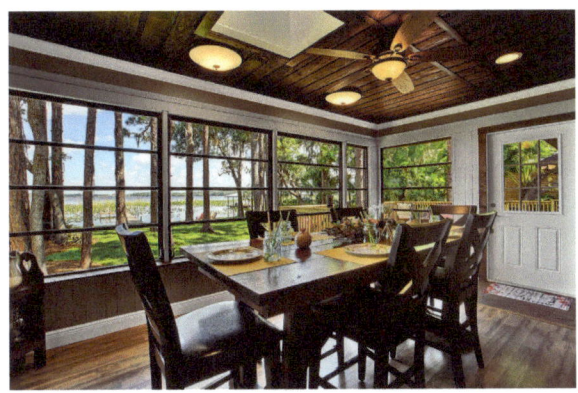

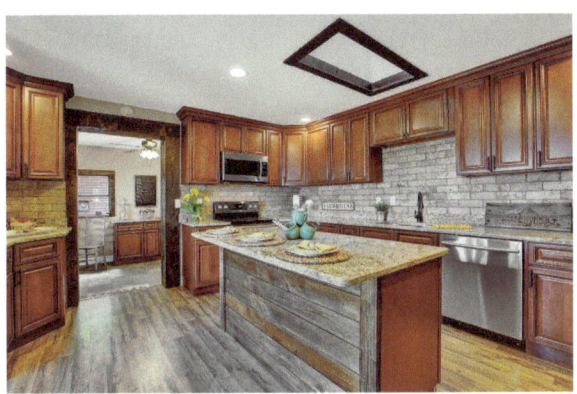

Whether a professional is used for staging or not, there are still things you and the seller can do to maximize the final product of the photos. Some of these include

- Replace burnt out lights
- Turn on ALL lights (even the small ones over the stove)
- Clear the driveway of cars and debris
- Put away toiletries, shampoo, and other items in the bathroom
- PUT THE TOILET SEAT DOWN!!!!!!!!!
- Put away trash cans
- Turn OFF ceiling fans
- Remove pets
- Open the blinds
- Turn off the TV

This list is not exhaustive, but hits a number of the major points. Combining these with performing an overall cleaning of the home will go a long way in staging the house for photos.

So, if I was to coach a seller on the "perfect" way to go about staging the house, what would I say? Well, it would go something like this. . . .

Hire a professional stager and cleaning company to prepare and stage the house. Schedule this to take place 2–3 days before the photo shoot. Depending on the home, 1 day might be enough, but others may need more. In any case, there should be NO work needed on the day of the shoot.

Then, once everything is done and the house is properly staged, GET OUT! Book a room at a hotel and stay there until after the photo shoot is complete. You have one chance at the first impression these photos will make, so don't risk messing it up by returning to the home before the shoot is complete. After all, this is a 6-figure transaction. It's worth the investment to do everything possible to get as much of an edge as possible.

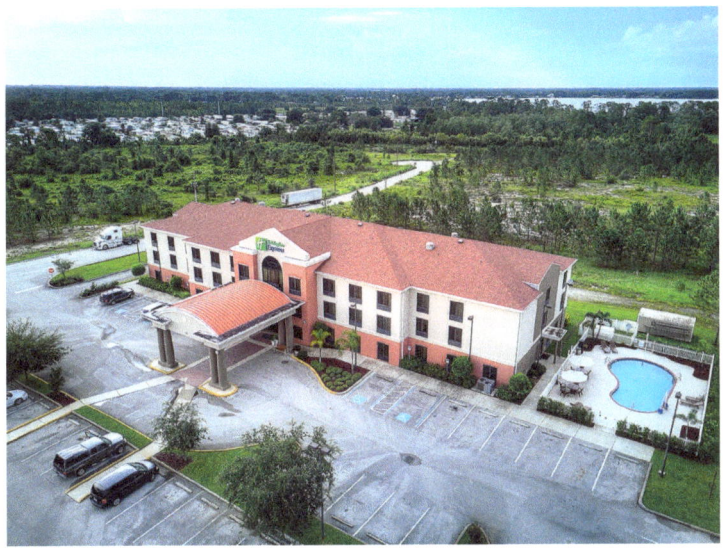

Of course, I understand that such a suggestion is probably laughable as few sellers would be willing to go to that extent (on their dime at least), but that would be the best way to handle the staging in a perfect world.

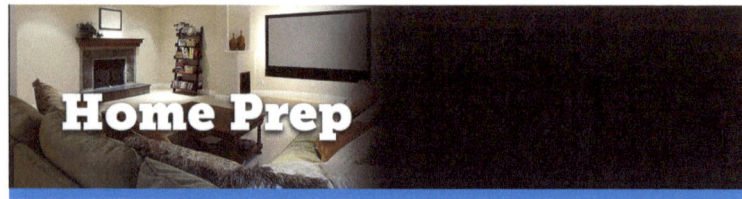

The following items are necessary to prepare the house for photo Shoot:

- [ ] Turn on all lights and lamps.
- [ ] Replace burned out light bulbs.
- [ ] Turn off ceiling fans.
- [ ] Make sure driveway is clear and free of cars and debris.
- [ ] Check house for cleanliness.
- [ ] Bathrooms - put away toiletries, shampoo, soap,toothbrush, toothpaste, towels.
- [ ] Kitchen - remove dishes from counter, garbage from trash can, clutter, magnets from refrigerator, and pet bowls.
- [ ] Remove clutter throughout the house.
- [ ] Put away high chair, booster seats, toys, etc.
- [ ] Store all workout and medical equipment.
- [ ] Make sure items stored under beds are not visible.
- [ ] Put pets away, out of photography areas.
- [ ] Have the yard mowed.
- [ ] Trim trees.
- [ ] Make sure leaves are blown.
- [ ] Put away all outside trash cans, recycle bins, water hoses, security signs.
- [ ] If there is a security fence around pool and you do not want it seen in photo, please remove security fence before photo shoot.
- [ ] Remove pool equipment from pool.
- [ ] If homeowner does not want child's name or personal photos shown, please take down before photo shoot.
- [ ] Take down holiday items so photos are not dated.
- [ ] For dusk shoot, please make sure there is a water hose at the property.

NOTE: On the day of the photography session, please arrive before the appointment to ensure home is ready to be photographed.

Prestige Aerial Services
863-451-3325
PrestigeAerialServices.com

36

WORK ALONE

If the sellers followed the advice presented at the end of the last chapter, this part should be easy. But considering that is not likely to happen. . . .

Whenever possible, you should take the pictures alone and with no distractions. While you should develop a systematic method to shooting the property, there will always be some art involved. The less distractions you face, the more likely you will stay in "the zone".

Distractions are only part of the problem when you're not working by yourself (these distractions are often the seller asking questions). The other issue is keeping other people out of the shot. If you're using the correct equipment, the angle of the lens will be wider than people are used to. They will think they are out of the shot, but they are not. Every time you stop to ask them to move, you lose your focus and it takes time to get it back.

In fairness, this is something you probably have little control over. If the seller wants to be present, it's their house. You'll just have to work with it and do the best you can. Most sellers understand the need to stay out of the way during a shoot and are very accommodating. Where they get in the way is normally just due to ignorance of what high quality equipment can capture (wide angle, view out the windows, and so forth). However, if you do have the choice, in most cases, you will maintain your focus and produce a better result in less time if you are working on your own during a standard real estate shoot.

VISUALIZE FUTURE EVENTS

Not we're starting to get into a little more of the art of the shoot. This would also be a reason to want to stay in your creative zone as you shoot the property.

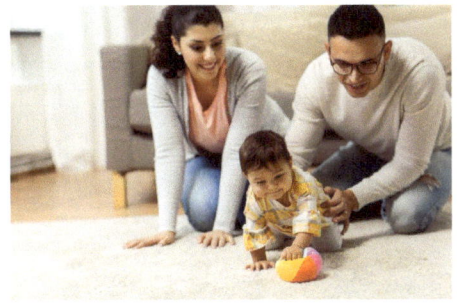

Many of the important events in a person's life will happen in a home. When taking the pictures, you want to be thinking of the events that will happen here and make it easy for the buyer to visualize themselves having these experiences.

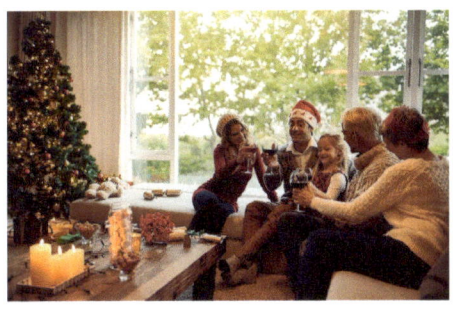

Remember, people make buying decisions with emotions and justify them with facts (not the other way around). Just like this is true when buying the latest iPhone, it's also true when someone buys a new home.

Think of events like Thanksgiving, Christmas, and so forth. What will be happening in the home on those days? What will people be doing? Where will they be? Actually, don't just think of them, imagine them. Try to make it real in your mind's eye. Then capture angles that show this.

Some of these angles might be the dining room table and how it extends to the kitchen, the living room where children might play Christmas morning and how it extends to the back yard, or any other countless possibilities.

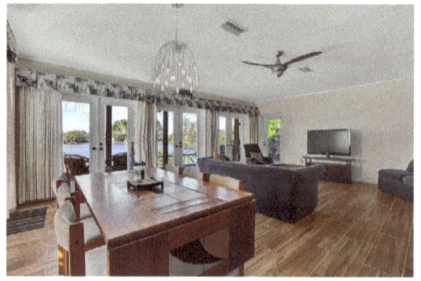 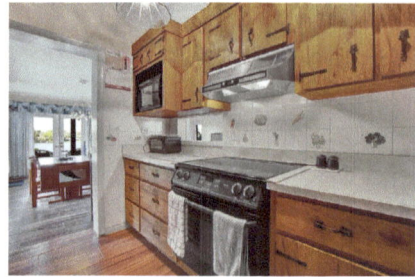

Remember, you're not snapping photos of a building. You're attempting to capture and tell the story of someone's dream—the dream of the person who will buy the house and make it a home.

PERFORM A WALK THROUGH

This is a critical ritual you need to have before starting a real estate photo shoot. Every single time I shoot a house, I start with a walk through. Ideally, YOU should do the walk through instead of someone giving you a tour (the sellers will often want to do this thinking it might add something if they point to the bathroom and tell you it's a bathroom—they mean well, so be polite).

The walkthrough is your time to focus your mind on the house. Use this time to get to know the house, get the feel of the house, think about who would want to buy the house.

Also pay attention to the layout. How many bedrooms are there? How many bathrooms? What other items of note do you need to pay attention to?

I also use this time for any last-minute MINOR staging items. Again, at this point, the property should already be staged, but minor adjustments that do not take any real time should still be done. For example, I will turn on all the lights, turn off all the paddle fans, and open the blinds while doing my walk through. If there are items that need to be moved and can be moved simply, I will do so during this time. Often, it's as simple as moving a soap dispenser into the sink so it does not show up in the photos.

At the end of the walkthrough, the house (lights, fans, blinds and all) should be ready for shooting and you should have a good "feel" for the property.

It may sound overly simple. It is simple. But do not skip this step!

TAKE A LOT OF PICTURES

Not too long ago, I was a client at a professional photo shoot to take pictures of my family (not something I do—I'm a real estate photographer). In the case I'm thinking of, we went to a large company (I think it was a franchise) and they had multiple photographers taking pictures of a bunch of families.

When our turn came up, it was obvious that the person with the camera was not anywhere near as skilled as some of those we had used in the past. There are some photographers that are true masters of their craft. They spend years developing their skills (and it shows when you watch them on a photo shoot). This person, was not one of them. All that said, when the job was done and delivered, I was thrilled with the result. It looked amazing. How could this be?

What the photographer lacked in skill and experience, he made up for in the sheer volume of photos taken. I don't remember how many photos our package included, but it was nothing too crazy for family pictures. However, during the shoot itself, the photographer shot photo after photo after photo. The volume of data collected was huge. Somehow, between the children crying and screaming, he managed to snap a photo at the moment that facial movement on my child looked like a smile and he did this again and again (seriously—the little dudes wouldn't stay still for a moment, but the end result makes the 2 toddlers look like perfectly well behaved angels).

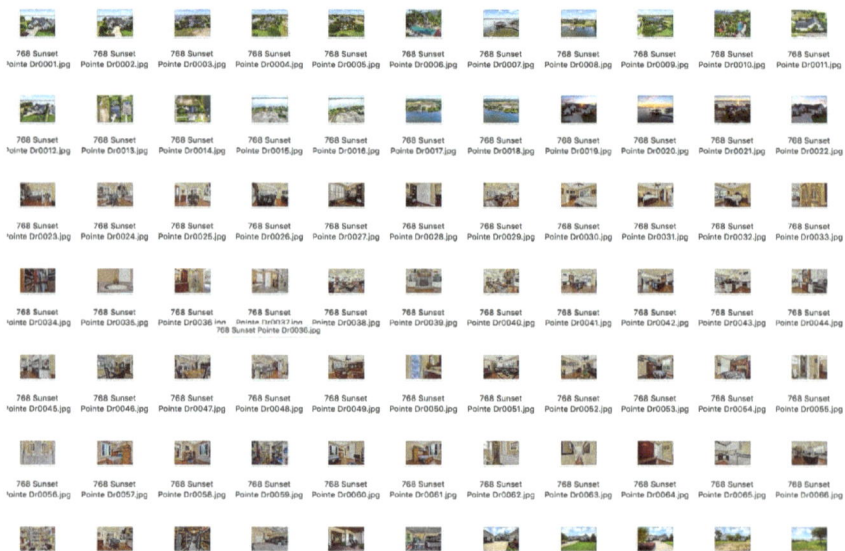

Several times a year, I'm normally teaching at events related to aerial and real estate photography around the county. A common question I get asked is how does someone new to taking real estate photos make sure that they get it right. My answer is always the same, take a lot of photos.

Taking a lot of photos is the best insurance against a shoot going bad that you can possible have. It doesn't mean you have to edit all of them. But if you have a large volume to select from, it is almost certain that you will find 20–30 really good ones to edit and use for the listing.

In time, as you become more experienced, you will be able to reduce the number of photos you take on site. However, even when you reach this level, I would still encourage you to lean more toward the generous side when taking photos. Why?

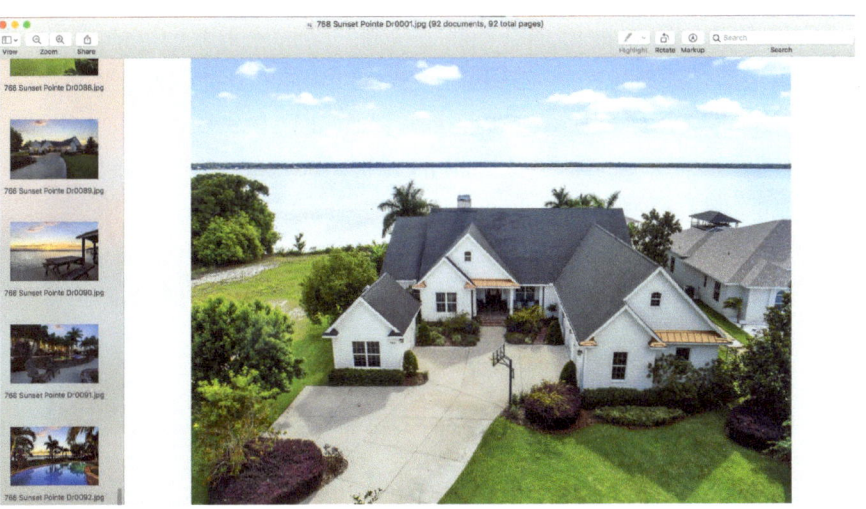

Some clients are very easy going and some will be very, very picky. If you deliver a photo taken from the right corner, they will want it from the left. In this example, how do you know which corner is the one the client wants the photo from? If everything else is equal, you won't. On top of that, sometimes you will be convinced the photo on the right is the better picture, but after delivery, they tell you they wanted the one on the left (they thought that would be better).

Now, if you only took one corner, even if you were "right" the client is not going to be happy. Now what do you do? Do you tell them "YOU'RE WRONG!"? Good luck ever getting hired again by that agent. Do you offer to go back and charge them for another shoot? That's an option, but if they truly believe that you messed up in the first place, they're going to feel nickeled and dimed and may not call you again. Do you go back and reshoot for free? I guess that's okay as long as it doesn't happen very often. It's definitely not cost effective.

All of the above contingency options would have simply been avoided by taking a photo from BOTH corners and delivering both. Using our example, if you did this, you would have spent just a few extra moments in the room shooting and the client would be happy because the specific angle they wanted would be present. Considering there seems to be a larger trend with real estate photographers to take less pictures, you will look like a rock star to your client and stand a good chance of being hired again and again.

Taking a lot of pictures is, by far, the best insurance policy you can put in place against a bad shoot.

USE A BUBBLE LEVEL

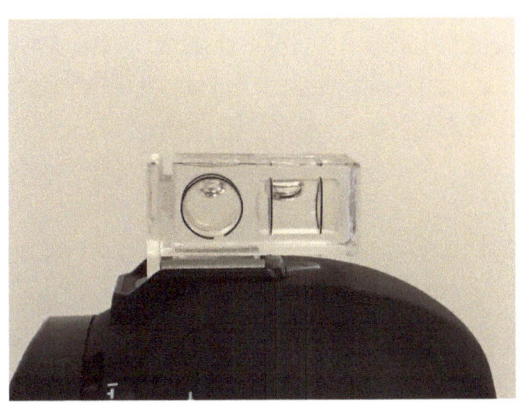

Every little advantage you can give your photos counts! Granted, some tiny advantages require large amounts of additional work and are thus not practical in many situations, but when you can get an edge with little to no additional effort, you need to take it.

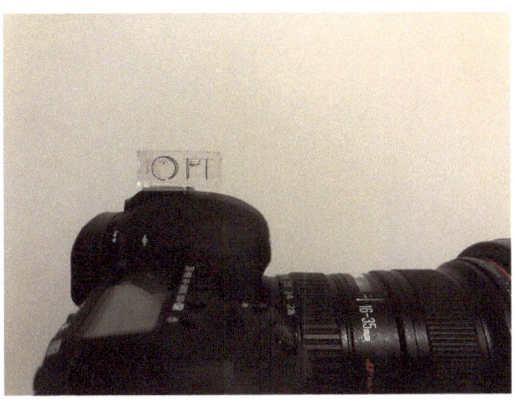

One of these edges is to make sure your photos are as level as possible. The obvious reason is you don't want the room crooked or sideways. But there is a larger reason.

One of the general objectives is to make the room look as large as possible. Therefore, you want every detail captured by your lens to show up in the photo in most cases. Yes, you can straighten a crooked photo in post-production. However, every time you do, you WILL lose some of the sides of the captured photo. Meaning, the more you straighten a photo in post, the smaller the room will appear.

The use of a bubble level is the most accurate way to know that your camera is level. After you frame each shot, look at the level and adjust as needed. Then make sure to look at how the shot is framed one more time to make sure you are framed correctly before taking the picture.

USE A HIGH-QUALITY LENS

I should probably start off and tell you that if you are using the kit lens that comes with the camera, STOP IT! If you're shooting with a DSLR (which you should be), you actually have 2 pieces of hardware to consider when making your purchase, the camera body and the lens.

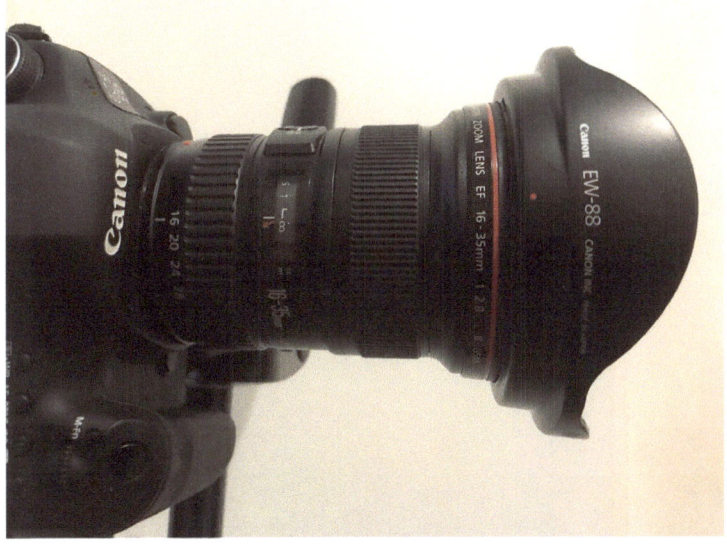

I understand that good camera equipment is expensive and sometimes there are budgetary concerns. If this is the case, you can save some money on the camera body. However, I suggest you do NOT pinch pennies on the camera lens.

The glass you put in front of your camera and quality of that glass will make a huge difference in the quality of the image you can create. The kit lenses are designed to be fairly cheap and are really there to get you into the camera. Considering that these photos are to sell 6 figure items, low quality is really not appropriate.

As of right now, I'm using a Canon EF 16-35 mm 2.8 L II USM lens. The camera you use will influence what lens you can put on it. Again, let me stress, the lens is not a place to pinch pennies. Spend the extra money and get a good, high quality lens.

USE A WIDE-ANGLE LENS

Your cell phone camera, while great for taking spur of the moment photos of friends and family, simply will not be able to capture anywhere near the amount in a room that the human eye can. Thus, you need to get a wide-angle lens.

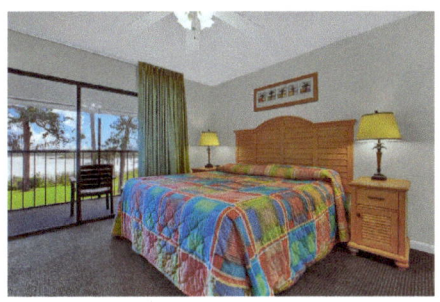

This is yet another reason why you cannot use the kit lens that comes with the camera. The lens is not wide enough for real estate photography. So, how wide should the lens be? Well, that depends on your camera.

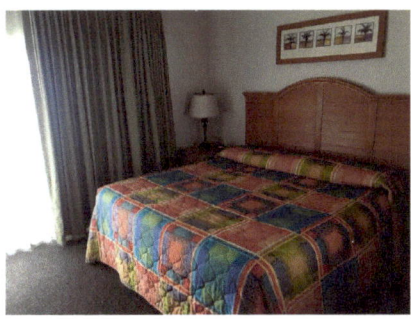

If you're using a full frame DSLR (which I highly recommend you do), you want the lens to go out to 16 mm. This will allow you to capture almost the same amount that the human eye will from end to end. It will allow the room to look large without going to the extreme (and even fake) effect of a fish eye lens.

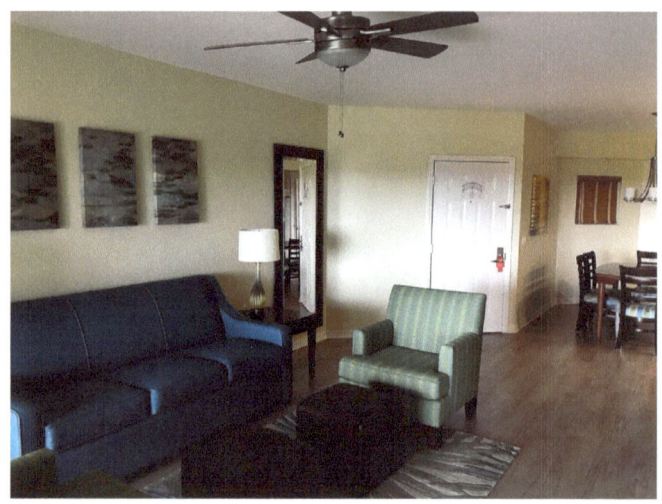

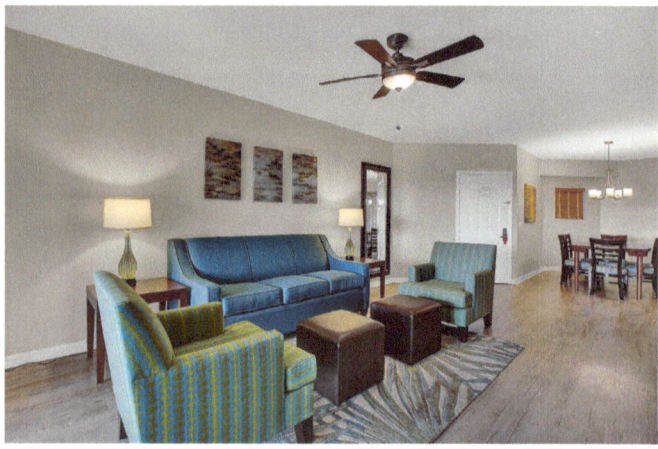

If not using a full frame DSLR, you need to account for the crop factor when picking the lens. In general, this means that if you are using a crop sensor DSLR (lower cost than a full frame), you will need to get a 10 mm lens. It's important to note that a 10 mm lens on a crop sensor DSLR is the same width as a 16 mm on a full frame DSLR.

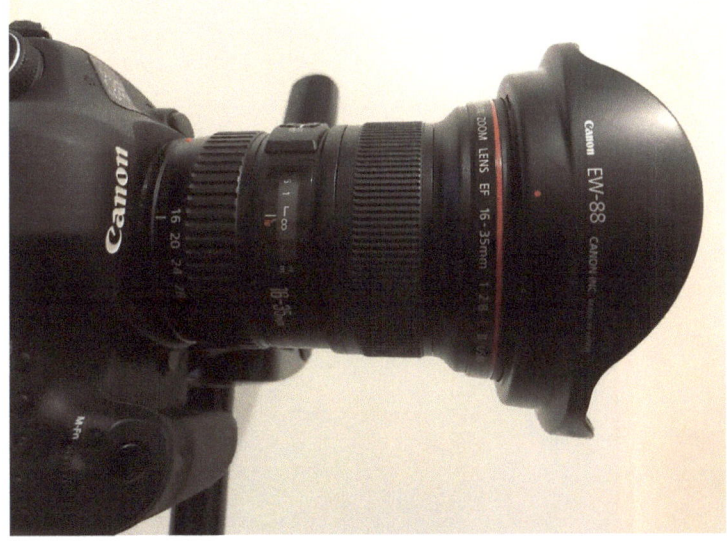

As stated in the previous chapter, I'm shooting with a full frame DSLR using a Canon EF 16-35 mm 2.8 L II USM lens. Most of the time, I have the lens zoomed all the way out to 16 mm.

STAY OUT OF THE PICTURES

Alright, the basics of this is pretty straightforward. Perhaps I should rewrite the title to state, "Double Check to Make Sure Your Reflection Is Not in The Picture."

There is no shortage of items in today's modern homes that would LOVE to capture your reflection and add it to you photo. Mirrors are obvious, but the real sneaky ones are stainless steel, glass, small mirrors inside cabinets, and even various objects around that house.

Whether you are a professional photographer or an agent wanting to take better pictures, having yourself or part of your equipment show up is a distraction that does not help the end result of making a buyer fall in love with the property. Every time you take a picture, you should scan the room checking for reflections—then check again. In fact, while my camera is taking its bracketed photos, I'm still looking back and forth to see if I've been caught in a reflection that I missed before I took the picture.

Bathrooms are universally difficult, but they are often the easiest to see the reflections as they are coming from standard mirrors. Be sure to watch the tile or shower door. Sometimes those will catch you. Options for these challenges are to pull the curtains shut or open the door if the shower has a glass door.

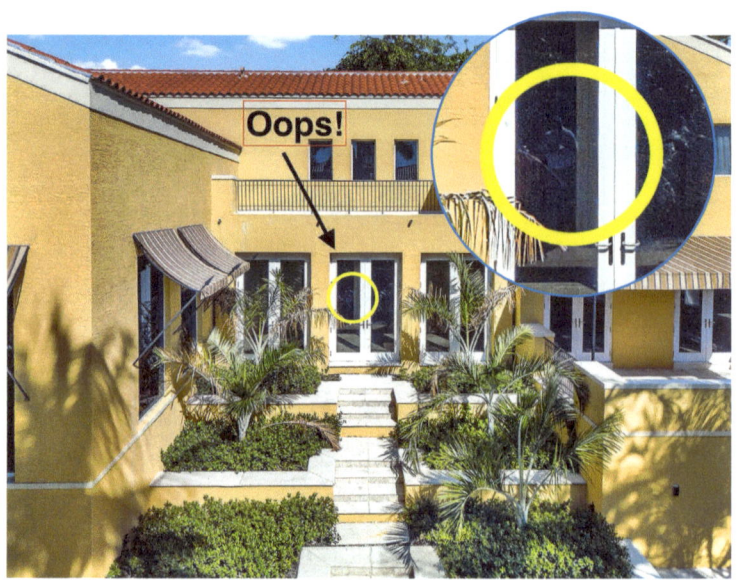

Kitchen stoves will often catch you by surprise. Watch the glass on the oven. The legs of the tripod often like to get caught in a reflection there.

Finally, exterior photos can catch you by surprise. Never take an exterior photo before looking at the windows for your reflection.

Often times, the object that is casting your reflection is small and, when looking through the view finder, can be hard to see. A simple trick that works well is it simply wave your arm while looking through the view finder. You may have a hard time seeing your image when you are perfectly still, but the motion of waving your arm will make it jump out. I've stopped myself from taking my own picture many times by performing this simple task.

No matter what you do, this will always remain a little tricky. This is why you need to give everything a final review before sending the photos to the client. Real life, if you take enough pictures, you'll show up in some. Not if, but WHEN it happens, take note of where and when this happened and you will quickly get better at anticipating where reflections are likely to catch you.

INCORPORATE EXTERIOR VIEWS

I want you to think of the exteriors in 2 ways. The most obvious is the exterior photos of the house, but the other way (and the main focus of this chapter) is to include exterior views when taking your interior photos.

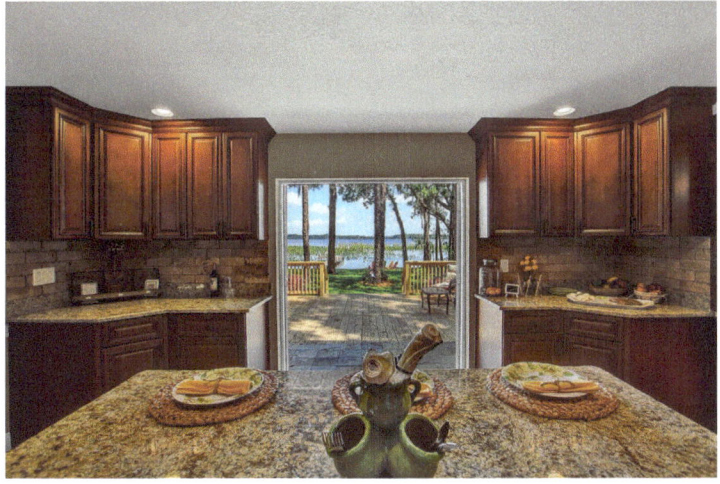

If you've been shooting with a cell phone or not bracketing your photos, you might not have given this a whole lot of thought. However, one of the advantages of taking bracketed photos is you will now get a good view of the inside of the house as well as a view out the windows.

This goes back to the idea of visualizing events and experiences. For example, if the house has a lake view, where will the home owner look at this view? Will they be standing or sitting? Inside or outside? Take the photo to show these angles. In addition, find angles of the rooms that also highlight the view out the windows. If the bedroom has a lake view, you should make sure some of your shots clearly shows both the bedroom and the lake.

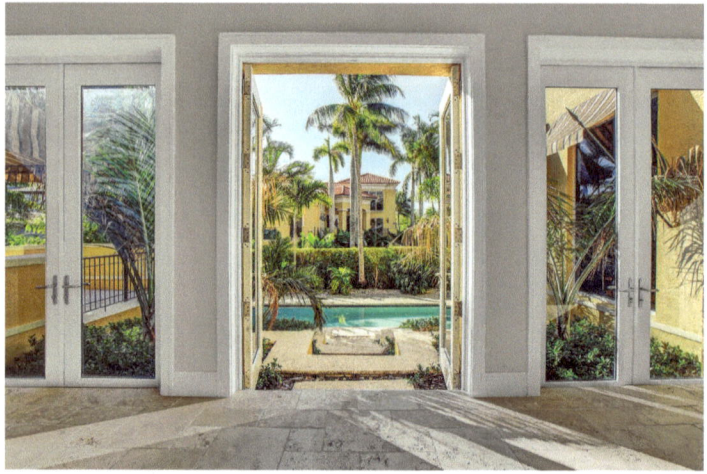

The general exterior photos are a little more straightforward, but there are still some things to consider.

First, watch out for the reflections (see the previous chapter). This will often be a problem when taking a photo of the front of the house. In a perfect world, you would normally have a front photo with the camera facing the center of the house at a 90-degree angle. In real life, this will often have you caught in a reflection. So, what do you do?

Move to one side or the other just enough to get out of the reflection. Once you do, it may be tempting to just take the picture with the camera pointed straight at the house and then crop it in post-production. Don't do this. Instead, angle the camera so the entire house is centered. Yes, the photo will be taken a bit from an angle. However, this is going to look better in the final version and it will be very rare that anyone will know that you are not taking a true straight on photo.

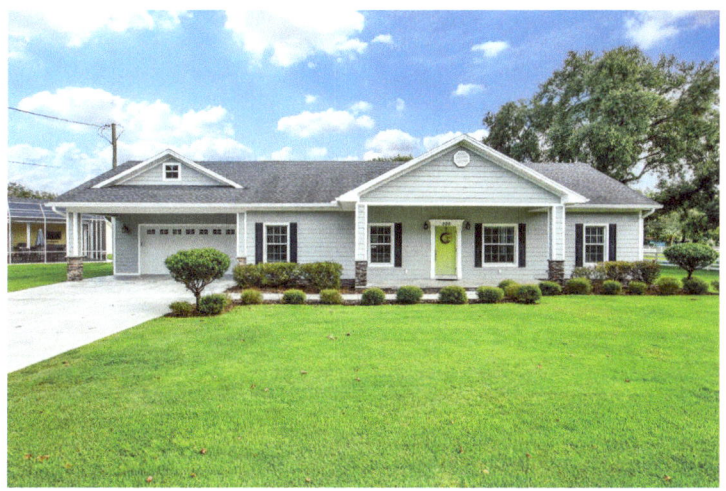

PREPROGRAM YOUR CAMERA

You're not going to need more than 2 or 3 camera setting set ups for your real estate shoots. As a result, it is a total waste of time (and thus money) to enter in ALL the settings every time you are going to shoot. Let the camera do this.

Again, perhaps your make and model does not allow this. If that's the case. . . . upgrade.

I have 2 standard camera settings based on if I am shooting inside or outside. My interior settings are in the C1 preset and the exterior settings are in the C2 preset.

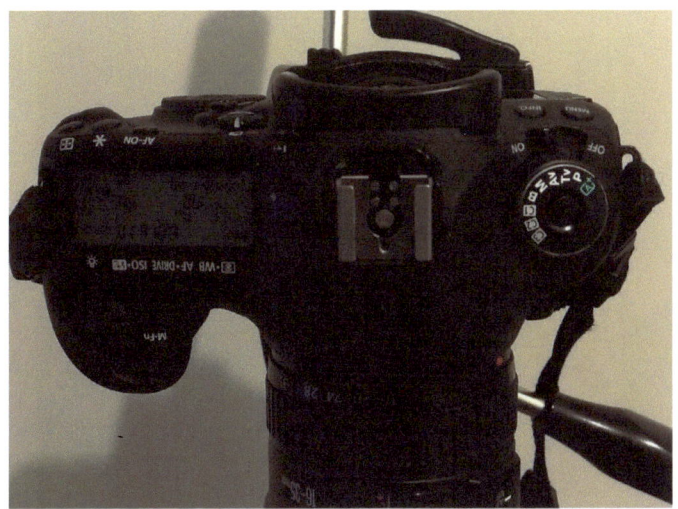

Along with saving time, this also makes training new photographers much easier as everything can focus on framing the shot. They don't need to know much of anything about camera settings because all of this is already programmed. They only need to know to turn the knob between C1 and C2.

SHOOT FROM THE CORNERS

As a general rule of thumb, the corners are going to going to give you your best angles to view the home. From the corners you can minimize dead space, see down hallways, see multiple views, and make the room look as large as possible. It is also a good way to create a systematic method for shooting the property.

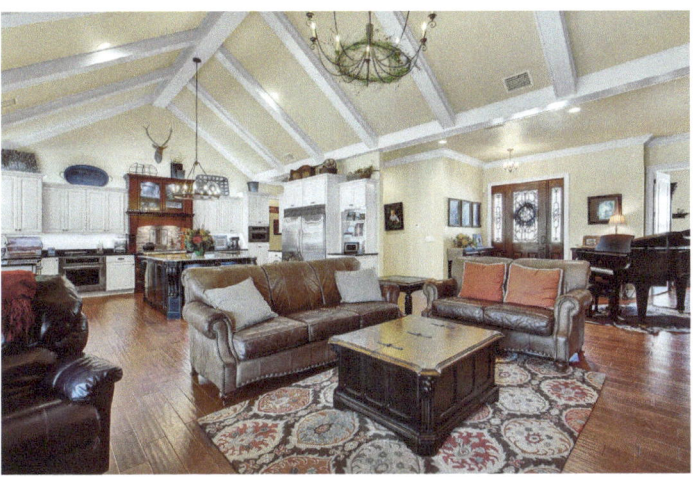

A good method that will help you with your angles and make sure you don't miss anything is to start with your first photo at the door, then make left turns throughout the house. Every time you come to a corner, stop and take a picture. Continue this throughout the house and you will normally have everything covered very well. If you'll do this when you're first starting, you are much more likely to produce a consistent result.

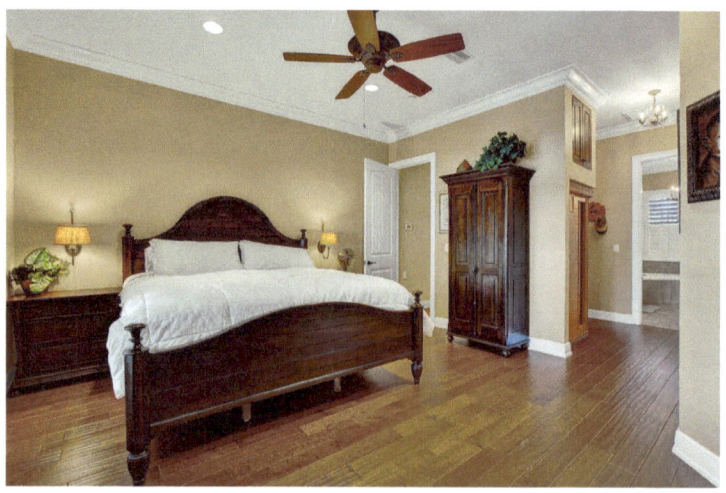

As you get a little more experienced, you will be able to reduce this somewhat. In general, I normally shoot every corner from the larger rooms, 2 corners in bedrooms, and 1 in normal sized bathrooms. I'd like to emphasize that this is what I NORMALLY do. Depending on the situation, I may deviate.

Here's a tip that will help give you an edge missed by many, look for hallways and other rooms that can be included with your corner shot to make the room look bigger. Again, this is an advantage of shooting from corners, it makes it a lot more natural to include this. If you can have the side of the photo show a hallway (more open space), even if it is just a sliver, the mind will pick up on it and the room will feel larger to the viewer. It's a little thing, but will go a long way in making your photos more effective.

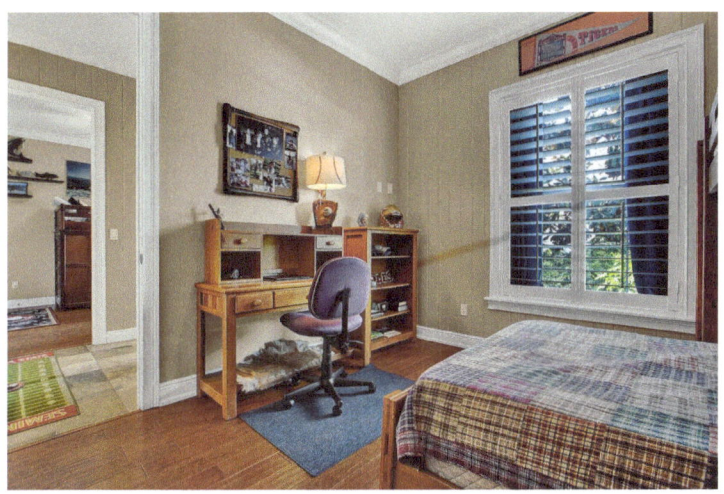

None of this is to say you should never shoot from a wall or somewhere other than a corner. Quite frankly, you should be looking for additional angles to show the home and make it emotionally interesting. If you have any doubt about whether a photo should be taken, TAKE THE PICTURE! Even if you're shooting a package that only includes a small number of photos, while on site, take the photo and figure out which ones will be edited in post-production. It is much more time and money effective to take the extra few second to take the photo and not need it than to not take it only to realize later the you actually did need it.

DON'T USE AN IPHONE

Along with iPhones, include any cell phone, standard (cheap) digital camera, iPads, tables, and so forth. USE PROFESSIONAL EQUIPMENT.

A little while ago I was having a conversation with one of my clients. Telling me of his experience, he told me that when meeting a possible new seller, he often simply pulls out his phone and opens his social media account. He then asks the seller if they want their photos to look like what you normally see online or like this (then he shows photos of his listings). The difference is immediate and is often enough to close the deal.

It's easy to quantify the average expectations when adding aerial photography and professional indoor HDR photography to a listing. Studies show that homes will sell 32% FASTER and for 5.25% MORE MONEY. What's a little harder to quantify is the benefit of getting more listings. However, this could actually be the biggest financial benefit of getting rid of the cell phone photos and doing professional photos.

At the time I write this, a quick Google search shows that the average home price is about $232,000. For simplicity, let's round that down to $200,000. If you're a real estate agent, how much do you make when you sell this home? Granted, it will vary based on the contract, commission splits, and so forth, but let's work with a 6% commission that is split between you and another agent. In this case, taking 3%, you make $6000.

Now, ask yourself this question, if you were to perform a professional photo shoot on EVERY property you list and use that as a selling point to distinguish you from your competition, do you think sellers would be more inclined to list with you verses the agent taking cell phone photos of the toilet with the seat up? If you only picked up 1 additional listing in a year, how many shoots would that extra $6000 pay for? I'll help you with the math, if you're in an area with $200,000 homes, you're probably looking at 24–40 FULL shoots paid for by that 1 extra listing (how many homes did you list last year?).

In addition, your commission checks will go up per the studies AND you'll have more time (the most valuable resource) because you're outsourcing the photos to someone else who specializes in the skill. This extra time can be spent doing what YOU do best (finding buyers for your listings, finding new sellers, and so forth). As all that time adds up and compounds, how do you think this will impact your bottom line?

All of these financial and time benefits are yours if you will simply put down the cell phone and use professional photography. Since the costs are covered by a single listing (and you can reasonably expect to pick up more once you start doing this), it doesn't really cost you ANYTHING to add this to your service. Rather, it's going to cost you if you don't.

ABOUT THE AUTHOR

PABLO TERREROS is the owner of Prestige Aerial Services, the premier aerial drone services company in Central Florida. He is also a commercial/instrument rated pilot and an active firefighter/paramedic in South Florida. Pablo's company, Prestige Aerial Services, is a member of the Sky Eye Network, the largest network of professional drone companies in the world, the Sebring Chamber of Commerce, and 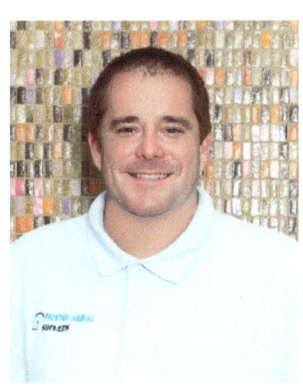 an affiliate member of the Heartland Association of Realtors. Through his company, he performs hundreds of real estate photo shoots each year in addition to other aerial drone services. Pablo also travels the country teaching new drone pilots how to get started in the drone industry of which real estate photography is often the first entry point.

For inquiries or to contact the author:

Pablo Terreros at pablo@prestigeaerialservices.com

Visit www.PrestigeAerialServices.com for more information